The Countries

Italy

Bob Italia

ABDO Publishing Company

visit us at
www.abdopub.com

Published by ABDO Publishing Company, 4940 Viking Drive, Edina, Minnesota 55435.
Copyright © 2002 by Abdo Consulting Group, Inc. International copyrights reserved in
all countries. No part of this book may be reproduced in any form without written
permission from the publisher.

Printed in the United States.

Photo Credits: Corbis
Art Direction & Maps: Neil Klinepier

Library of Congress Cataloging-in-Publication Data

Italia, Bob, 1955-
 Italy / Bob Italia.
  p. cm. -- (Countries)
 Includes index.
 Summary: An introduction to the history, geography, people, economy, transportation,
communications, and social life and customs of Italy.
 ISBN 1-57765-754-3
  1. Italy--Juvenile literature. [1. Italy.] I. Title. II. Series.

DG417 .I83 2002
945--dc21
                                                          2001045854

Contents

Ciao!

Hello from Italy, a country known for its rich history and natural beauty.

The Etruscans were one of the first peoples to settle in Italy. But it was the Romans who established a great empire. After Germanic tribes brought the empire to an end, Italy did not regain its glory until the **Renaissance**. In modern times, Italy struggled through two world wars before it became an **economic** success.

Italy has a varied landscape, with mountains, plains, and a moderate climate. It also has a variety of plants and animals.

Most of Italy's people are **ethnic** Italians who practice the Roman Catholic religion. Many of Italy's national holidays are tied to the Roman Catholic religion.

Most Italians live in cities. They enjoy a healthy **economy** based on industry, much of which is owned by Italy's government. Italy's largest cities are Rome, Milan, and Naples. Each has modern transportation and communication systems.

For centuries, Italians have made important contributions to the arts. Today, Italy remains one of the world's greatest **cultural** centers.

Ciao *from Italy!*

Fast Facts

ROME ★

OFFICIAL NAME: Repubblica Italiana (Italian Republic)
CAPITAL: Rome

LAND
- Mountain Ranges: The Alps, the Apennines
- Highest Peak: Monte Bianco 15,771 feet (4,807 m)
- Major Rivers: Po, Tiber, Adige

PEOPLE
- Population: 57,092,000 (2002 est.)
- Major Cities: Rome, Milan, Naples
- Language: Italian
- Religions: Roman Catholicism, Protestantism, Islam, Judaism

GOVERNMENT
- Form: Parliamentary democracy
- Head of State: President
- Head of Government: Prime minister
- Legislature: Parliament
- National Anthem: "Fratelli d'Italia" ("Brothers of Italy")

ECONOMY
- Agricultural Products: Grapes, wheat, olives, corn, oranges, tomatoes; cattle, hogs
- Manufactured Products: Clothing and shoes, foods and beverages, motor vehicles, petroleum products, machinery, chemicals
- Mining Products: Natural gas, granite, marble
- Money: Lira and euro (100 centesimi = 1 lira; 100 cents = 1 euro)

Italy's flag

Italian lira

Timeline

800 B.C.	Etruscans migrate from the east to Etruria
500s	Etruscan kings rule Rome
200s	Rome begins its empire, controls Etruria
100s	Roman Empire controls all Mediterranean lands
A.D. 400s	Roman Empire falls to the Germanic tribes
800	Charlemagne is crowned emperor after organizing the Germanic tribes
1100s	City-states form in northern Italy
1400s	Renaissance begins
Early 1800s	Napoleon Bonaparte captures Italy
1861	King Victor Emmanuel II unites most of Italy
Early 1920s	Benito Mussolini takes control of Italy
Early 1940s	Italy fights against the Allies during World War II
1943	Mussolini is overthown
1946	Italy abolishes the monarchy
1947	Italy adopts a new constitution
1981	Republican Party leader Giovanni Spadolini becomes prime minister
1984	Government ends a 1929 law that made Roman Catholicism Italy's state religion
2001	Silvio Berlusconi becomes Italy's prime minister

History

The Etruscans were one of the first peoples to settle in Italy. About 800 B.C., they **migrated** from the east to Etruria, which includes the present-day Tuscany, Umbria, and Latium regions in Italy.

Etruscan kings ruled Rome during the 500s B.C. Rome grew from a shepherd's village into a powerful city under these kings. Etruria came under the control of Rome early in the 200s B.C.

Charlemagne conquers Rome

The ancient Roman emperors began building their empire during the 200s B.C. By the A.D. 100s, the Roman Empire controlled all of the Mediterranean lands and influenced the **culture** of the many groups of people it ruled.

In the A.D. 400s, Rome fell to Germanic tribes such as the Lombards, Franks, Saracens, Germans, and Normans. After organizing these tribes, Charlemagne was crowned emperor in 800.

Italy fell into a period called the **Dark Ages** until the 12th century. Then powerful **city-states** formed in the north. This led to the **Renaissance** of the 15th century. Artists, **architects**, philosophers, and sculptors created many masterpieces during this period. Spanish and Austrian empires controlled Italy during the next centuries.

Napoleon Bonaparte captured the region in the early 1800s, and made it part of his French empire. Then in 1861, King Victor Emmanuel II united most of Italy into one country.

Benito Mussolini, a **Fascist dictator**, took control of Italy in the early 1920s. Italy joined the **Axis Powers** during World War II and fought the **Allied**

Benito Mussolini

nations. In 1943, Mussolini was overthrown because of Italy's troubles in the war.

In 1946, the Italians voted to abolish the **monarchy**. They elected an **assembly** which adopted a **constitution** in 1947. Alcide De Gasperi, a member of the Christian **Democratic** Party, became **prime minister**.

In 1981, **Republican** Party leader Giovanni Spadolini became prime minister. He was the first Italian prime minister since the end of World War II who was not a Christian Democrat.

Bettino Craxi of the **Socialist** Party became prime minister in 1983. The next year, the government decided to end a 1929 law that made Roman Catholicism Italy's state religion. In 1986, the government convicted 338 people of belonging to the Mafia, a criminal organization in Sicily.

Christian Democrats held the office of prime minister from 1987 to 1992. From 1992 to 1994, non-Christian **Democrats** held power. For the rest of the decade, different **coalitions** controlled Italy's government. Then in 2001, the House of Liberties came to power. Silvio Berlusconi became Italy's **prime minister.**

Since World War II, Italy has developed one of Western Europe's most successful **economies**. Today, northern Italy is one of Europe's wealthiest and most modern regions.

Silvio Berlusconi

The Land

Italy has eight land regions. These regions include the Alpine Slope, the Po Valley, the Adriatic Plain, the Apennines, Apulia and the Southeastern Plains, the Western Uplands and Plains, Sicily, and Sardinia.

The Alpine Slope is in northern Italy. It has tall mountains and deep valleys. Monte Bianco, Italy's highest peak, is located here. The Po Valley stretches between the Apennine Mountains and the Alps. Melting mountain snows feed into the Po River, Italy's longest, which runs through the valley's center.

The Adriatic Plain is north of the Adriatic Sea, and features a limestone **plateau**. The Apennines stretch almost the entire length of Italy. These steep mountains have soft, eroded rock.

Apulia and the Southeastern Plains make up the famous heel of the boot-shaped Italian **peninsula**. This region's plateaus form steep cliffs along the Mediterranean Sea.

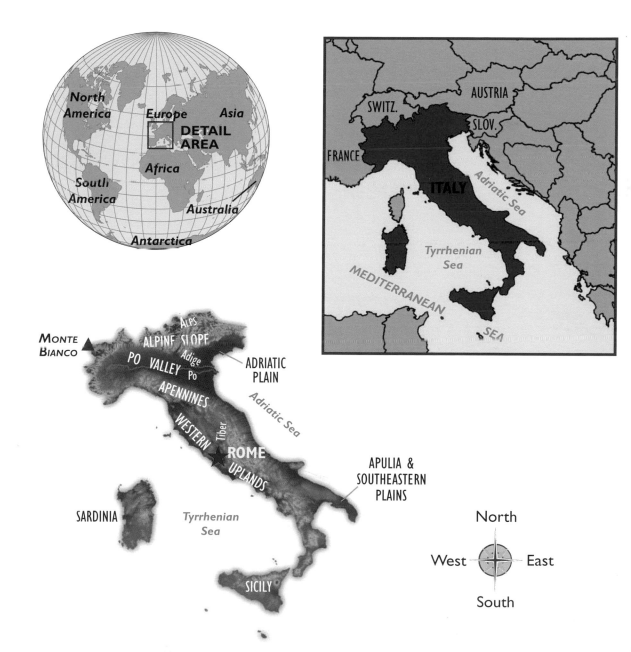

North America
Europe
Asia
DETAIL AREA
Africa
South America
Australia
Antarctica

SWITZ.
AUSTRIA
FRANCE
SLOV.
ITALY
Adriatic Sea
Tyrrhenian Sea
MEDITERRANEAN SEA

ALPS
ALPINE SLOPE
MONTE BIANCO
Adige
PO VALLEY
Po
ADRIATIC PLAIN
APENNINES
Adriatic Sea
WESTERN
Tiber
ROME
UPLANDS
APULIA & SOUTHEASTERN PLAINS
SARDINIA
Tyrrhenian Sea
SICILY

North
West
East
South

The Western Uplands and Plains stretch along the Tyrrhenian Sea. This region has fertile agricultural lands.

Sicily, the largest island in the Mediterranean Sea, has plains and mountains. Its famous Mount Etna is Europe's highest active volcano. In the Tyrrhenian Sea lies the island of Sardinia. It has mountains and high **plateaus**.

Italy has a moderate climate. Spring, summer, and fall are usually sunny and dry. Along its coast, the days are usually warm. Italy's winter is often rainy, cool, and cloudy. Snow falls in the Alps and the Apennines.

Mount Etna

Rain

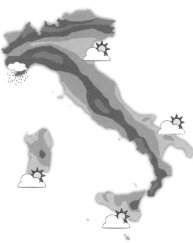

AVERAGE YEARLY RAINFALL

Inches		_Centimeters_
Under 8		Under 20
30 - 40		75 - 100
40 - 60		100 - 150
Over 60		Over 150

North
West — East
South

AVERAGE TEMPERATURE

Fahrenheit		_Celsius_
Over 75°		Over 24°
68° - 75°		20° - 24°
61° - 68°		16° - 20°
55° - 61°		13° - 16°
46° - 55°		8° - 13°
39° - 46°		4° - 8°
32° - 39°		0° - 4°
Below 32°		Below 0°

Summer

Winter

Plants & Animals

Italy has a variety of plants and animals. Forests of beech, oak, and chestnut trees grow at the lower levels of Italy's mountains. The middle levels feature grasslands, and beech and **conifer** forests. Only low bushes grow at the highest elevations.

Foxes and wolves roam throughout many regions. Chamois, ibex, elk, reindeer, and several other kinds of deer live in the high mountains.

Seals live off the seacoasts. Other wild animals in these areas include badgers, hare, hedgehogs, lemmings, otters, and wild boar. There are also eagles, falcons, owls, storks, thrushes, and many other birds common to Europe.

Fish are plentiful off the coasts. Anchovies, sardines, shrimp, and tuna are common in these waters.

A chamois

Italians

Most of Italy's people are **ethnic** Italians. Ethnic Germans live in the region bordering Austria. Ethnic Slovenes live along the border of Italy and Slovenia. And ethnic French people live in the region near Italy's border with France and Switzerland.

Most people in Italy live in cities, in concrete apartment buildings. Only the wealthy live in single-family homes. The poorest neighborhoods are often found along the edge of a city. In rural areas, single-family homes are more common.

A narrow city street lined with apartment buildings

Italian is the official language of Italy. Standard Italian **evolved** from a Tuscan dialect. It is used in public schools and in radio and television. Some people still speak different regional dialects.

Life in Italy differs from north to south. The north has more money, more cities, and more industry. The south is poorer, with an **economy** based on agriculture.

All Italian children from age 6 to 14 must attend a five-year elementary school, and a three-year junior high school. Then they may attend one of many different high schools, including technical schools, **vocational** schools, science schools, classical schools, teacher training schools, and language schools.

Most people in Italy are Roman Catholics. Smaller religious groups include Protestants, Muslims, and Jews.

Italy is famous for its **unique** foods, which vary from region to region. The north is known for its pasta and cream sauces. The south is known for macaroni and tomato sauces. A famous Italian dish is *risotto*, a rice dish with vegetables. Italy is also known for its cheeses.

Italians often eat their main meal at midday. Pasta, veal, pork, fish, and pizza are popular. Sometimes, *antipasti* (appetizers) are served before the main meal. Fresh fruit is a popular dessert. Wine is served at almost every meal, except breakfast.

A pizza maker works in his kitchen

Biscotti
An Italian cookie

- 5 cups all-purpose flour
- 1 1/2 cups sifted confectioners' sugar
- 2 tablespoons baking powder

- 1 cup shortening
- 3 eggs
- 1 tablespoon vanilla extract

Sift flour and measure. Resift with sugar and baking powder onto a flat surface. Cut shortening into dry ingredients until mixture resembles coarse cornmeal. Make a well in the flour and break eggs into it. Add vanilla and knead dough well for about 5 minutes until it is smooth, adding a little more flour if dough seems too soft and sticky. Pinch off bits of dough about the size of an apricot, and form into desired shapes. Place one inch apart on greased cookie sheet and bake in hot 450-degree F (230-degree C) oven for 10 minutes, until golden brown. Watch carefully, because they burn easily.

AN IMPORTANT NOTE TO THE CHEF: Always have an adult help with the preparation and cooking of food. Never use kitchen utensils or appliances without adult permission and supervision.

English	Italian
Yes	Si (SEE)
No	No (NOH)
Thank you	Grazie (GRAH-zee)
Please	Favore (fah-VOR-ay)
Hello	Ciao (CHOW)
Goodbye	Arrivederci (uh-ree-vah-DAIR-chee)

LANGUAGE

The Economy

Northern Italy is among the most advanced industrial areas of Western Europe. Southern Italy relies on agriculture, so it has less industry.

Italy's government owns a large part of many companies. And it controls all energy production from **petroleum** and natural gas. Still, Italy depends on exports from other countries for its energy supply.

About 50 million **tourists** visit Italy each year. So restaurants and hotels are leaders in Italy's service industry.

Manufacturing is an important part of Italy's **economy**. Clothing, **textiles**, processed foods, petroleum products, electrical and nonelectrical machinery, automobiles, and chemicals are the country's main products.

Grapes are Italy's most important agricultural product. Most grapes are used to make its world-famous wines. Italy is also one of the world's largest producers of sugar beets and artichokes.

Italy has few natural resources. Natural gas, marble, and granite are Italy's most important resources.

A hillside village and vineyards in Tuscany, Italy's top wine-producing region

Historic Cities

Italy's largest cities are Rome, Milan, and Naples. Each has more than a million people.

Rome is Italy's capital. It has been an important center of civilization for more than 2,000 years. Because of its long history, Rome is called the Eternal City. It has churches, palaces, and ancient buildings and monuments. Rome is also one of the world's **cultural** centers. Vatican City, the spiritual and governmental center of the Roman Catholic Church, is located within the city. But Vatican City is independent from Italy.

An aerial view of the Tiber River in Rome

The Galleria Vittorio Emanuele II in Milan

Most modern Romans earn their living through government or service industry jobs. **Tourism** also provides a large part of the city's income.

Milan is Italy's second-largest city. It is Italy's center of finance, manufacturing, and international trade. Advertising, publishing, and design and fashion industries are centered in this city. Italy's stock market is also located here.

Milan is the industrial center of Italy. It has thousands of factories and several large manufacturing plants. The plants produce chemicals, electric appliances, **textiles**, tires, and transportation equipment. Though it has many modern buildings, Milan is also known for its ancient structures, including the Sforza Castle.

Naples is Italy's third-largest city and another major manufacturing center. Manufacturers make automobiles, cement, chemical products, locomotives, office machinery, ships, and textiles. **Tourism** is also an important industry in Naples. People come to see Naples' scenery and historic churches and castles. Mount Vesuvius, the only active volcano on Europe's mainland, is just 7 miles (11 km) from the city.

Opposite page: The city of Naples along Naples Bay and beneath Mount Vesuvius

Transportation & Communication

Italy has a modern road system. Superhighways run the length of the country. Tunnels carved through the Alps link Italy's highway system to those of neighboring countries.

Trains are also an important way of traveling through Italy. Railways connect all of Italy's major cities. And a high-speed train travels between Rome, Florence, and Milan.

People walk along the platform between trains in the train station in Parma, Italy.

A newsstand in the Piazza Farnese in Rome

The Leonardo da Vinci International Airport near Rome is Italy's busiest airport. Milan also has an international airport. The national airline is Alitalia.

Shipping is an important way of transporting goods in the north. Canals link the Po River with many northern lakes.

Italy has 450 television stations, 1,000 radio stations, and 70 newspapers. Half of all Italians own televisions.

Government

Italy's government is a **parliamentary democracy**. It has a president, a **cabinet**, a parliament, and a **prime minister**.

The president is the head of state. He or she chooses the prime minister. The president can break up the parliament and call for new elections. The president is also the commander of the Italian armed forces, and can declare war.

The cabinet is called the Council of Ministers. It is led by a prime minister, who chooses its members. The prime minister is the head of government. He or she forms the government and determines national policy.

The parliament is made up of a senate and a Chamber of Deputies. Both houses of Parliament pass laws and elect Italy's president to a seven-year term.

Italy is divided into large governmental units called regions. Then each region is divided into **provinces**. Each province is broken into many **communes**.

The Italian Parliament

Holidays & Festivals

Italy has many national holidays tied to the Roman Catholic religion. The feast of the Epiphany is held on January 6. Italians also celebrate the Immaculate Conception on December 8, All Saints' Day on November 1, Christmas Day on December 25, and St. Stephen's Day on December 26.

Italy also has many nonreligious national holidays. Liberation Day on April 25 celebrates the Italian liberation from Nazi-**Fascist** occupation in World War II. The Anniversary of the **Republic** on June 2 celebrates the proclamation of the Italian republic.

Many rural festivals celebrate harvest, food, and country, such as spring fairs in Piedmont and Lombardy. The May music festival is held in Florence.

People going to Christmas Mass at St. Peter's Basilica in Rome

Sports & Leisure

Soccer is the most popular sport in Italy. Every major city has a professional soccer team. Some cities also have professional basketball teams. Other sports popular in Italy include fishing, hunting, cycling, roller-skating, and baseball.

Three boys run after the ball at a soccer game in Pisa.

The Colosseum

Many Italians like taking a traditional Sunday *passeggiata,* or family stroll. They often take trips to the mountains or seashore. Watching television is also a popular pastime.

Italy is one of the world's greatest **cultural** centers. Some of its museums, like the Pitti Palace and the Uffizi Palace in Florence, are famous worldwide. **Artifacts** from Italy's earliest history can be seen in its national archaeological museums. Rome is famous for its ancient ruins, including the Colosseum.

Leonardo da Vinci

Michelangelo

For centuries, Italians have made important contributions to the arts. During the **Renaissance**, Italy produced some of the greatest painters, writers, sculptors, and **architects** in history.

In the late 1200s, Giotto became one of the world's most influential artists. Leonardo da Vinci became famous in the 1400s. Raphael and Michelangelo came along later in the Renaissance. Michelangelo was also a great sculptor.

Three great Italian writers of the 1300s were Dante, Petrarch, and Giovanni Boccaccio. And St. Peter's Basilica, designed by Donato Bramante, became the greatest example of Italian Renaissance architecture.

Italian composers wrote the first operas in Florence in the 1590s. Important Italian composers include Alessandro Scarlatti and Antonio Vivaldi.

In modern times, Italians have made their mark on the motion-picture industry. During the 1950s and 1960s, Gina Lollobrigida, Sophia Loren, and Marcello Mastroianni became movie stars. Michelangelo Antonioni and Federico Fellini established themselves as great movie directors. Important modern authors include novelist Italo Calvino and Nobel Prize-winning playwright Dario Fo.

Film director Federico Fellini on the Pont Sant Angelo in Rome

Glossary

allies - countries that agree to help each other in times of need. During World War II, Great Britain, France, the United States, and the Soviet Union were called the Allies.

architecture - the art or science of planning and designing buildings.

artifact - anything made by human skill or work a long time ago.

assembly - a group of people gathered together for some purpose.

Axis Powers - During World War II, Germany, Italy, and Japan were called the Axis Powers.

cabinet - a group of advisers chosen by the prime minister to lead government departments.

city-state - a state consisting of a city and its surrounding territory.

coalition - when two or more countries work together toward a common cause.

commune - the smallest district in a country.

conifer - a tree or shrub that has cones.

constitution - the laws that govern a country.

culture - the customs, arts, and tools of a nation or people at a certain time.

Dark Ages - a period in the Middle Ages (A.D. 400s to the 900s) characterized by a lack of education, the loss of artistic and technical skills, population decrease, and primitive economic life.

democracy - a government that is run by the people who live under it.

dictator - a ruler who has complete control and usually governs in a cruel or unfair way.

economy - the way a nation uses its money, goods, and natural resources.

ethnic - a way to describe a group of people who have the same race, nationality, or culture.

evolution - gradual development.

fascism - a political philosophy that favors a dictatorship, and places nation or race above individual rights.

migrate - to move from one place to settle in another.

monarchy - a government controlled by a king or queen.

parliament - the highest lawmaking body of some governments.

peninsula - land that sticks out into water and is connected to a larger land mass.

petroleum - a thick, yellowish-black oil. It is the source of gasoline.

plateau - a raised area of flat land.

prime minister - the highest-ranked member of some governments.

province - one of the main divisions of a country.

Renaissance - a revival of art and learning that began in Italy during the fourteenth century, marked by a renewed interest in Greek and Latin literature and art.

republic - a government in which its citizens elect representatives to manage the government, which is usually headed by a president.

socialism - a kind of economy. The government or the citizens control the production and distribution of goods.

textile - of or having to do with the designing, manufacturing, or producing of woven fabric.

tourism - the act of traveling for pleasure. A person who does this is called a tourist.

unique - being the only one of its kind.

vocational - of or relating to training in a skill or trade to be pursued as a career.

Web Sites

Tour Italy
http://touritaly.org
This fact-filled site will take readers on virtual tours of Italy's famous places.

Roman Empire
http://www.roman-empire.net/children/index.html
This interactive site offers fun information about the Roman Empire. Readers can learn how Romans dressed, what they ate, and take a virtual trip to Ancient Rome!

These sites are subject to change. Go to your favorite search engine and type in Italy for more sites.

Index